THE STORY OF MY CHILDHOOD

by
Ida Lantto Schroeder

Pyramid
Publishers
1314 Grandview Circle
Buffalo, MN 55313
763-486-2867
www.pyramidpublishers.com

Printed by Lightning Source 1246 Heil Quaker Blvd. La Vergne, TN USA 37086
ISBN – 978-0-9851514-8-5
Library of Congress Control Number: 2016956267
[Copyright Designation if there is one other than the above]

Cover and Interior Design and Layout by Just Ink Digital Design
Printed in the United States of America

INTRODUCTION

My mother, Ida Lantto Schroeder, born on June 22, 1906 above the Lantto store in West Albion, MN, wrote down her childhood memories at age 70 after being encouraged to do so over several years by myself and others. By the time she passed away on May 19, 1996, one month before her 90th birthday, she had enjoyed a long and fruitful life, spanning from the horse and buggy days to the space age and cell phones. Her story here delightfully captures several brief moments of those very early years.

The scenes depicted carry us back to a happy time, as we see a seemingly carefree young girl filled with humor and a zest for life. But the carefree days came to an abrupt end at her age 12, when her mother prematurely passed away. Events took an awful turn in the Fall of 1918 when the Spanish Influenza pandemic raged through not only her community, but also worldwide. I recall her telling how her father, Jacob, on a cold November day, wrapped up her sick mother, Olga Mary, in several blankets for warmth and drove her in the new 1918 Model T Ford (with side curtains) from the farm just south of French Lake to the Cokato hospital, never to have her return. I did not realize until very recently, while going through Mother's genealogy, that Olga Mary was very pregnant on that fateful ride with about-to-be born little Eddie. Mother had always said that her mother had died of the flu during the big epidemic. I am under the impression that Olga Mary died that very first night in the Cokato hospital. Later I realized that neither Olga Mary nor baby Eddie survived that night, and one report listed Olga Mary as dying in childbirth at age 35 on November 4, 1918.

Mother never got over the death of her mother, and throughout her life she would relate to me how much she still missed her mother. She would periodically bring up anecdotal stories to me about life with her mother. The last and most dramatic story Mother told me about her mother related how Mother, while sitting outdoors and enjoying the warm morning sun in her yard at her first retirement home at a log cabin on Tozer Lake, Spooner, Wisconsin, saw her mother, Olga Mary, standing there right in front of her and some 50 years after Olga Mary's death, and she said words to the effect: "It's all right, Ida. Yes, it's me. I'm fine, and everything is going to turn out okay." Then she disappeared, leaving Mother with a warm, comforted and joyous glow, as she described it to me.

Mother's parents were both born in Finland, and migrated to the United States with their respective parents in the late 1800's. Many Finnish families settled in Wright County, Minnesota, and were the early settlers in communities like Annandale, West Albion, French Lake and Cokato. Her father, Jacob Lantto, at age 30 married Olga Mary Mattson, at age 19 in Annandale on February 2, 1903. In the early years, they lived above Jacob's corner store in West Albion, where Mother was born. Jacob's and Olga Mary's respective lineages are illustrated in the genealogy sections at the end of this book. I found Olga Mary's genealogy difficult to trace, while Jacob's was much easier, traceable back to 1590. When I would inquire of Mother as to where in Finland her parents originated, she would relate the cities of Oulu, Tornio and Muonio, although rarely mentioning Muonio, and not differentiating which parent came from which city. As you can see from the genealogy sections, Jacob's ancestors go back a long ways from Muonio, a small town in Lapland and above the Arctic Circle on the Sweden/Finland border, and from Ylimuonio, just north of Muonio. As an aside, Muonio fell upon recent hard times when, except for the historic main church (Muonio Kirkko) which was left intact, the whole town was totally destroyed by the exiting Nazis during World War II*. Muonio is in the heart of Lapland, and the Laplanders, or Saami (also Sami), are considered the indigenous population of the area, although apparently the Saami prefer not to be referred to as Laplanders.** On the other hand, I do not know which of Olga Mary's parents came from Oulu, or which came from Tornio. Those of you readers who know more about our Finnish cousins and ancestors than I do can better answer that question.

Curious to define my own heritage, I submitted a DNA sample to National Geographic's Genographic Project. The results on my mother's side indicate a first reference population "...based on samples collected from people native to Finland", and also indicate a dominant 57% Northern European component that "...likely reflects the earliest settlers in Europe, hunter-gatherers who arrived there more than 35,000 years ago", with a Northeast Asian component which "...reflects mixing with native Siberian populations, particularly the reindeer-herding Saami people of far northern Scandinavia."*** I would encourage the reader to research his/her own genealogy, along with the origins and long history of the Saami people.

Thomas P. Schroeder

*Wikipedia
**Wikipedia
***Genographic Project, National Geographic

THE STORY OF MY CHILDHOOD

The first memories of my childhood began at about the age of three when we were living at the Jacobson place, so-called in honor of the previous owner.

My father[1] had owned a general merchandise store out in the country[2]. That is where I was born on June 22, 1906. My older sister and brother[3] were born there, too. Our mother[4] didn't like it there because we lived upstairs over the store. It wasn't home to her. She wanted a house, a yard, gardens and chickens. So my father sold the store and bought a small farm about two miles from town.

[1] Jacob Lantto
[2] West Albion, MN
[3] Lillian and Alfred
[4] Olga Mary Mattson Lantto

*****

I remember on a summer day my sister, brother and I were sitting at the hayloft door with our bare feet dangling down when my Godfather drove into the yard in a horse and buggy and a bag of candy for me. In later years, my sister related how they were lucky to get one piece of that candy.

*****

During the summer months my sister and I washed our hair every day at the windmill close to the kitchen door. Our legs were so short that we'd set the basin of water on the ground, bend over, and soap our hair and slush around in the suds.

*****

One Christmas comes to my mind. The tree was standing in a corner of the living room and was gaily decorated with burning candles and draped with strings of little candies. I remember standing in the corner behind the tree with my hands hanging down behind me, touching nothing, but my mouth was nibbling on the string of candy. That evening Santa Claus came and brought us a brand new baby sister.[5]

*****

My older sister, brother and I often went visiting our closest neighbors, the Johnsons. One afternoon we went there expecting to get the usual warm welcome, but both Mr. and Mrs. confronted us with fierce and angry looks. We saw broken dishes all over the floor. We didn't even get to say 'hello' as we just turned around and ran. We didn't dare go there for a long time.

[5] Mildred

We often went into the apple orchard and sat under the apple trees, just sitting there and talking.

We lived there, I think, for about four years. Then my father found a bigger and better place. It was close to the general merchandise store where we three oldest were born. This was in the fall of the year. The people living there could not move until spring, but we had to move. So my father built a one-room cabin, solid, with windows on the south side and a door on one end. He had plans to use it later as a chicken house. We lived in this future chicken house all winter. My brother would wake up in the morning and sing "cock-a-doodle-doo." We girls would go cackling around like chickens. That kept us amused all winter. This place we called "The Laurie Place" in honor of the previous owner. They finally moved away, and we finally moved in, so thankful to get away from the cramped little chicken coop, as we were to call our home of one winter.

Long after we moved into the big house and the chickens moved into the little house, I'd go there to visit them, housecleaning for them or just sitting by the heater watching them being so busy scratching around in the clean straw on the floor.

My fondest memories of my childhood are of the Laurie place. My mother was happy there. She got her house, yard, gardens and chickens. I guess her happiness rubbed off on us because we were happy, too. It was there that I met my first very own friend, Lida, who lived on the adjoining farm. We were inseparable, and like two peas in a pod. We could talk, laugh, giggle and be silly to our hearts' content. We once overheard my mother saying to her mother that "…they have to have fun, too." So we went on having our fun. There was an old tumbled down house between my house and hers. We called it 'Our Haunted House.' We spent many happy hours there, running up and down the rickety stairs, in and out of the rooms, pretending we heard ghosts.

*****

One day after the noon meal (which we called dinner), I slipped outside trying to keep the dish washing out of my mind. I stayed and stayed outside a long time. Finally, I said to myself: "Might as well go do those old dishes." I went in the kitchen, where no one was around, and no dishes sitting around waiting for me to do. I just couldn't believe my eyes. Finally it dawned on me that mother had done them. How happy that made me. No one else ever said anything about it, but I did feel terribly guilty for a long time.

*****

We churned our own butter at the well. Just before it turned into butter, we would spread some on bread and top it with sugar. That was a real treat.

*****

There was an unfinished room over the dining room which we called 'the attic.' I would climb up there and spend hours just being by myself reading, rather looking at some old books. I called it my secret room.

*****

I had a doll with a China head. By every Christmas that head was broken, and every Christmas I'd get a new head for it, and never a whole new doll.

*****

The haystacks were fun to play around, as were the strawstacks. The haystacks near the barn looked very inviting to me one day, so I climbed up and slid down, running my hand along the sides. I felt a zing in my right hand. When I got to the ground, my hand was all bloody, with a deep cut in it. I had to run to the house for mother to fix it. There had been a long-handled spear standing up against the haystack. Mother explained how it could have been worse, so there was no more sliding in haystacks or strawstacks for me.

*****

Mother sent me to the store one day, which was close by, and formerly owned by my father, but was then owned by his brother, my uncle. She didn't give me a written list because I couldn't read anyway (this was before starting school). She just told me what to get. When I got to the store, my mind was a blank. For the life of me, I couldn't remember what I was supposed to get. My uncle had things to do in the store room, so he said he'd come back a little later. I just stood there and stood there trying to rack my brain. When he came back to see if I could remember, my mind was still a blank. He suggested that I use the phone and call home. I did, and that solved the problem.

*****

Oh yes, we had a phone now. I well remember the day it was installed. Now I could call up Lida and she could call me.

✶✶✶✶✶

One day we had a terrible scare. My father was burning weeds and rubbish in the old hayfield below the house. I thought the flames were very scary, and evidently so did my younger brother. The first thing we noticed was that our father wasn't around. We called and called for him, running every which way looking for him. We looked all over outdoors, in the barn, in the sheds, and even towards the fire. Then we went to look for him in the house: upstairs, basement, closets, and in just about every corner. Finally, someone stumbled upon him behind the door to the downstairs bedroom in a closet-like place, sound asleep! By now we all were so tired and worn out and hysterical when we saw that he was safe that we just collapsed, crying.

✶✶✶✶✶

Peddlers were common in those days. A pair of them, a man and a woman, stopped at our house one day. They were traveling on foot, with each one carrying a heavy bag of merchandise on the back. We were just ready to sit down for supper, so my mother invited them to supper, too. We had apple sauce for dessert, but the man ate his apple sauce before his dinner. I looked at my brother, and he looked at me, with great wonder in our expressions as much to say: "What! Eating his dessert first! Who ever heard of that?" I guess he saw the exchange of thoughts because he said: "I want to be sure to have my dessert, so I'll eat it first." The woman was all tired out from walking with that heavy bag on her back and she felt rather sick, so mother asked them to stay all night. No more beds were available, so they slept on some quilts on the living room floor. The next day they left. I was glad because I was afraid of peddlers.

✶✶✶✶✶

We went sliding down the hill close by and skating in the ditch close by. My brother got a new sled for Christmas. My sister and I

12

asked to slide down the hill with it. He said it was okay if we didn't break it. Down the hill we went, but bumped into something and it broke. We never used his sled again.

*****

My brother took to snaring rabbits during the winter months. He sold the hides to the store close by. He wanted me to go with him to check the snares, so every morning before school, in the bitter cold, we'd make the rounds of the snares.

*****

There was a bull fight one summer day in the pasture below our sliding hill. Such roaring and bellering. We all ran to see what was going on. The bull from across the road had come over to take out his grudges on our bull and in our pasture. No one dared go near, so we just stood there watching them. Finally, the neighbor's bull ran out of grudges and went back into his own pasture.

*****

Every summer on Midsummer's Day, June 24th, there was a community picnic in our spacious yard under the trees. Ice cream, pop and gum were sold, and people bought their own box lunches. At one picnic, the ice cream didn't taste very good. It must have been made from spoiled milk. No one complained, and they kept on buying ice cream cones, and so did I. I don't recall how many I ate but, at the end of the day, I became very sick. It all came up, and then I felt better. The day after those picnics I would go scanning the picnic grounds for money, and invariably I would find a nickel or a dime.

While I was still believing in Santa Claus, I did find myself on one Christmas wondering how come Santa's handwriting was like Mother's. While peeling potatoes with Mother for dinner, I said that Alfred (my brother) had said that there is no Santa Claus. She said that he was only fooling. When the teacher came back from her Christmas vacation, she said there were Santas on every street corner collecting money. Now I was really confused, as I had thought there was only one Santa!

Mother played the organ, and often sang in her beautiful high soprano voice. That was the music at our house. However, Grandma had a Victrola with a horn on it. We'd play all her records all day long when we went there.

We lived about a third of a mile from school. The teacher always boarded at our house. This pleased me because she often wiped the dishes for mother, and I got out of it.

I was old enough to go to school by now. I could hardly wait for the first day to come along. Well, it did, but I couldn't go. I had become violently ill to my stomach from eating too many apple peelings the day before, when mother was canning apples. Before the day was over, I had gotten over it. By the time the kids and the teacher were due home, I was sitting up in the apple tree by the house. The teacher grinned and said: "They all got so far ahead of you that you'll never catch up." That definitely cured me. I went to school the next day.

One day in school my tooth hurt slightly, not much, but I made believe it was a terrible toothache. I said nothing, but put my head down with the tooth-ache side on the cool desk. The teacher finally noticed me, and asked if I wanted to go home. Of course I did! I went home and told my mother why. She told me to lie down on the couch. I did for awhile, but soon forgot about the toothache and began to monkey around. Mother noticed this and said: "If you feel so good, you can go back to school." Back to the couch for me for the rest of the day. There was no more toothache for me.

*****

The first movie I ever saw was at the schoolhouse. Father took us older kids with him. All I can remember about it was some 'darkies' were stealing chickens from a chicken house. That sure was exciting. When we got home, we burst into the house all excited, saying: "We saw some chicken thieves." Mother tried to hush, hush us because the baby might wake up, but we could hardly settle down.

*****

One day, the teacher who was boarding at our house was up in her room correcting papers. My sister and I went up to see her. We were standing beside her desk when I noticed something right on the edge of her desk beside me that looked like a stick of gum. When no one was looking, I snitched it. On our way down the stairs, I put it into my mouth. It turned out to be a rubber erasure.

*****

I never did go to the third grade. When I got that far, I was the only one in that grade, so the teacher put me into the fourth grade. I seemed to make it alright, as I went into the fifth grade the next year.

There was always a program and a basket social at Christmas time to which the public was invited. That one year the teacher let the older pupils go home early, and kept the little ones for a party because they wouldn't be able to come in the evening. I was one of the older pupils, but I volunteered to stay so my younger sister and brother could walk home with me, and not alone. I stayed and had a real good time. I also had to be there in the evening, so I got in on two parties. I always liked my teachers and I always liked school. On Saturdays and vacations I'd always be playing school by myself.

In the spring the 'rubber ice' was fun to walk on. The ice had started to melt and was sort of wiggly. One afternoon I walked home from school alone. I stopped to look at the rubber ice in the ditch along the way. I touched it with my hand, then my foot, and finally with both feet. I started walking on it, but down I went up to my knees in the water. I splashed out and went home in a hurry and into the living room to dry out by the coal stove. I told no one; therefore, I didn't get bawled out.

When I got far enough in arithmetic for the problem solving, I just could never get it. I could add, subtract, multiply and divide, but problem solving was something else. It just wasn't my line. Every day I had to stay after school to try to finish my arithmetic. This one time, having no idea how to solve it as usual, I added, subtracted, multiplied and divided until I got the answer in the back of the book. The teacher came to see how I was doing. She could hardly suppress a smile while saying a long "no-o-o-o." So she told me to go home and we'd take it up the next day in class.

*****

I was getting pretty big by then. Grandma wanted me to come stay at their house during the summer months. They lived on a lake shore. Grandpa went fishing often, and took me with him with my little bamboo pole. He taught me a lot of fishing tricks. Grandpa was a real companion. He always listened to kid talk, looking right at you with his smiling face.

This one summer I didn't go stay at Grandma's. Right in the middle of summer we got a phone call saying that Grandpa had died suddenly. We went to the funeral. Grandpa was gone. No more Grandpa. It was terrible for me.

*****

The following summer my uncle bought his first car, a Maxwell. He took Grandma, a neighbor Grandma and me for a ride. The neighbor Grandma had never had a ride in a car before. She was afraid, and began to yell: "You are going so fast!" The more she yelled, the faster my uncle drove, which was 25 miles an hour. The roads then weren't flat like today, so we went whizzing along up the hills and down the hills, much like today's roller coaster. It sure was fun for me.

*****

We lived at the Laurie place for about five years. My father came home one day and said he'd found a bigger and better farm for us. The thoughts of going someplace else was exciting, but to leave my friends at school, and to leave Lida, was unbearable. However, we moved. We always called the new home 'The Rouseau Place' in honor of the previous owner. The first thing we girls did was to climb up into the attic. Mrs. Rouseau had said that we could have the things they'd left up there. We spent hours up there playing dress-up with the old clothes. Henceforth, that was where I played school. We soon found

17

new friends at school and just loved the teacher, who taught there three years instead of the traditional two. We didn't board the teacher anymore because there were other families closer to school.

*****

My sister and I had a playhouse in the corncrib. One day my sister was the hostess and I came to call on her. She greeted me politely and asked me to sit down. I did, and took up the newspaper to read. After a bit she said to me that you are suppose to talk, too. So I laid down the paper and proceeded to talk. We had a pleasant visit. We were busy playing house one day when we noticed our father peeking at us through the boards. Who knows how long he'd been there. When he saw we'd spied him, he went off laughing.

*****

An epidemic of diphtheria had swept into the community. We all had it, including me. Each family was quarantined for about six weeks, but I was for 10 weeks due to the fact that I couldn't, or wouldn't, gargle like the rest. I was put into a room upstairs with the door locked, and a blanket dipped in an antiseptic hung on the outside of the room. I went in and out through the window unto a ladder outside the house, as this was upstairs. One night a terrific thunderstorm shook the house and broke the window. My mother wanted to come up and get me, and to heck with diphtheria. But my father said that she isn't moving around so she must be asleep. And asleep I was, so soundly that I never heard the storm. In the morning, the broken window more than surprised me. I couldn't imagine how that had happened. The news of the storm amazed me.

*****

Everyone was buying a Model T Ford, so my father bought one, too. It was a touring car with side curtains for when it rained. Now it didn't take so long to get to Grandma's, to my aunt's, and to anywhere else. The horse and buggy days were left behind during the summer. But for the winter there was still the sleigh and horses.

*****

We still didn't have electricity, as there was no rural electrification yet. Two of the families got Delco motors and made their electricity. We were still using kerosene lamps. My father had running water put into the kitchen, pumped by a windmill, but no sewer going out. We had an outside toilet. For bathing purposes, we had what was called a 'sauna.' It was a two-room cabin close to the house. One room was for bathing. There was a fire box which heated the rocks and heated the water. Steam for heat was made by throwing a dipper of water on the hot rocks. The other room was the dressing room.

*****

While getting ready to go to Grandma's for one more summer, I told mother that I didn't want to go. She said I'd better go. It was lonesome there with no other kids to talk to or play with. She was thinking of Grandma there all alone all day long. My uncle was gone all day. I, too, realized this and so I went. But I said to my sister: "Well, I don't care. Anyway, I don't have to do anything, just sit and lie in the hammock." This wasn't quite true, for I did help Grandma a lot. After spending most of my summers there, Grandma's began to feel like a second home. To this day I think fondly of Grandma's. Of course, Grandma has been gone long since, but my uncle still lives there with his family.

*****

After I got home from Grandma's that last summer, it was State Fair time. My father went every year. When we kids were old enough, he took us one at a time each year. Now it was my turn. I talked my mother into going along, and so she went, too. We went with the new Model T Ford. It was nice to whiz along so fast. We even stayed all night in a hotel room, and got back the next evening. We not only took in the State Fair, but we also went sight-seeing and visited some friends. Oh yes, we went to a movie and saw "The World War." This was in the first part of September, 1918. World War I came to an end two months later, on November 11th. It was the last time that mother went anywhere. I was always glad that she had the chance to go to Minneapolis, as she hadn't been there for 15 years.

*****

No sooner had school started when the Spanish Influenza epidemic began to rage all over the country. We all came down with it. We brought all the beds downstairs. This way it was easier to care for each other. Besides, the upstairs was too cold. Schools were closed for two months. People had to stay in the house. Doctors warned people not to go outside. Some neighbors who were not sick came and took care of the stock. People were dying right and left. In one neighborhood family four grown-ups died in one day. We were on a phone party-line, so whenever the phone rang we took to listening in to find out who had died next. No funerals were allowed. The bodies were buried but the funerals were held later. My mother was taken to the hospital, and we never saw her again. Two months later we went to her funeral service. It didn't seem at all like she was dead. It was more like she was away visiting and would be home soon. More than once I caught myself saying that when mom comes home I'll tell her this and tell her that, and suddenly realizing that she wasn't coming home at all. My sister and I had to take over caring for the family and doing the housework. So I grew up in a hurry. That was the end of my childhood.

Jacob and Olga Mary Lantto wedding
February 2, 1903

Jacob Lantto farm (The Rouseau Place)

Jacob Lantto's hay loft and haystacks

Ida at age 13 in 1919

Teenage Ida

A young Ida

Ida at age 19 in 1925

Ida at age 28 in 1934

Ida's wedding photo

Ida at age 37 in 1943

Ida's family
Bill, Tom, Mary Lou, Jane, Husband Francis, Ida and Jim
1944

Ida's adult children
Left to Right: Bill, Mary Lou, Jim, Jane and Tom
1987

*Ida enjoying the warm morning sun
at Tozer Lake, Spooner, Wisc. - 1968*

Ida at age 87 - 1993

Ida's Children, Grandchildren and Great Grandchildren - 1998

<u>*Front Row*</u>: *Cathleen O'Donnell, Katie Barnes, Emily Parsons, Molly Parsons, Matt O'Donnell, Nick Schroeder, Drew O'Donnell, Sandi O'Donnell Robb, Margaret Parsons, Courtenay Schroeder*

<u>*2nd Row*</u>: *Mary Frances Schroeder Barnes, Anna Rose Barnes, Alan Barnes, Carmon Schroeder, Betty Huseby Schroeder, JoAnn Scapanski Schroeder, Duncan Robb, Terry O'Donnell Parsons, Henry Parsons, Marshall Parsons, Lindsay Schroeder, Cathy Schroeder Worley, Cindy Schroeder, Michael Worley, Kevin Schroeder*

<u>*3rd Row*</u>: *Rick O'Donnell, Mary Lou Schroeder O'Donnell, James Schroeder, Jane Schroeder Lawrence, Joe Lawrence, Michael O'Donnell, Carol Lynn Schroeder*

<u>*Back Row*</u>: *Jimmy Schroeder, Steve Horning, Jennifer Schroeder Horning, Lori Schroeder Waddick, Patrick Waddick, Peter Lawrence, Tom Schroeder, Bill Schroeder*

<u>*Missing from Photo*</u>: *Michele Schroeder, Daniel Tejada Schroeder, Jeanne Schroeder Robeshaw, Scott Schroeder*

Lantto Family Reunion
Annandale City Park – 1984

Jacob Lantto's Family – 1948

Front row: Mark Lantto, Beatrice Lantto Lusti, uncertain, Jackie Walker, Mildred Lantto, Maki Walker, Betty Lantto Lambert, Calvin Lantto

Second Row: Kenneth Lantto, Jacob's 2nd wife Anna, Lillian Lantto Barberg, Viola Matsen, uncertain, ElaineTormanen Lantto, Reino Lantto

Back Row: Wayne Barberg, Alfred Lantto, Erving Lantto, uncertain, Ida Lantto Schroeder, Harold Matsen, uncertain, uncertain, Leo Lantto

*Jacob Lantto's Mother, Maria Lovisa Jerisjarvi Lantto
with Second Husband Jacob Jacobson*

Olga Mary Mattson Lantto's Mother,
Beatrice Sophia Backman Mattson
(aka Grandma Mattson; aka Grandma Davidson)

1918 Model T Ford Touring with Side Curtains

The Muonio Kirkko

Drawing of central Oulu, Finland from the 19th Century
by J. Bostrom
Lithography from "Finland framstalldt i teckningar" 1845-52

Drawing of Tornio, Finland - 1908
by Alexander Federley

Ida Lantto Schroeder's Father's (Jacob Lantto) Paternal Genealogy (Nine Generations)

1) Niilo Kokko
>   b.   circa 1650
>   d.   date and location unknown

Children:
Niilo Kokko

2) Niilo Kokko
>   b.   1679
>   d.   July 2, 1739

Children:
Mats Nilsson Kokkoi

3) Mats Nilsson Kokkoi
>   b.   circa 1700
>   d.   date and location unknown
>   m.   Anna
>>   b.   est. 1663-1721
>>   d.   date and location unknown

Children:
Mikko Matsson Kokkoi

4) Mikko Matsson Kokkoi
>   b.   December 26, 1721
>   d.   June 24, 1773
>   m.   Brita Jonsdotter Niemi
>>   b.   1722
>>   d.   date and location unknown

Her Father: Jons Jonsson Niemi

    b. 1685

    d. Nov. 8, 1772, Muonio, Finland

Her Mother: Anna Olofdotter

    b. est. 1656-1716

    d. date and location unknown

Children:

Matts Mickelsson Kokko

5) Matts Mickelsson Kokko

    b. 1753

    d. Aug. 12, 1824 in Ylimuonio, Muonionniska fs, Finland

m. Ella Olofsdotter

    b. est. 1716-1774

    d. unknown

m. Valborg Jonsdotter Back

    b. Nov. 22, 1759

    d. March 3, 1843 in Ylimuoinio, Muonionniska fs, Finland

Her Father: Jons Henriksson Back

    b. est. 1694-1754

    d. unknown

Her Mother: Valborg Henriksdotter Katkasuando

    b. est. 1694-1754

    d. unknown

    Her father: Henrik Hansson Katkasuando

        b. circa 1667, Katkasuando, Muonio

        d. 1734, Muonen Niska, Overtornio, Finland

        His father: Hans Anundsson

            b. 1650 in Muonionniska, Finland

Children from Ella Olofsdotter:

a) Brita Mattsdotter Kokko

    b. Nov. 25, 1775

    d. unknown

Children from Valborg Jonsdotter Back:
a) Kristiina Mattsdotter Kokko
   b. May 12, 1785
b) Johan Mattsson Makikokko
   b. 1790
c) Abram Mattsson Makikokko
   b. 1792
d) Isak Gustaf Mattsson Makikokko
   b. 1794
e) Aron Mattsson Saarenmaa/Kongasenjarvi
   b. Aug. 7, 1799 in Muonio, Finland

6) Johan Mattsson Makikokko
b. 1790
d. Aug. 16, 1825 in Ylimuonio, Muonionniska fs, Finland
m. Brita Claesdotter Vuopio
Children:
a) Johan Alexanderi Johanson Makikokko Lantto
   b. June 7, 1819, Ylimuonio, Muonionniska fs, Finland

7) Johan Alexanderi Johanson Makikokko Lantto
b. June 7, 1819, Ylimuonio, Muonionniska fs, Finland
d. April 25, 1856, Ylimuonio, Muonionniska fs, Finland
m. Anna Margareta Andersdotter Narva
   b. Nov. 10, 1812, Mertajarvi, Karesundo fs, Sweden
   d. Aug. 3, 1895, Muonio fs, Finland
   Her father: Anders Johanssen Narva
      b. Dec. 26, 1779, Mertajarvi, Enontekio fs, Sweden
      d. Jan. 1, 1842, Mertajarvi, Karesuando fs, Sweden
   Her mother: Anna Salomonsdotter Tornberg
      b. Dec. 1, 1777, Konkama, Enontekio fs, Sweden
      d. March 31, 1858

Children:
- a) Johan Matthias Lantto
  - b. Feb. 28, 1841, Ylimuoniuo, Finland
- b) Maria Karolina Grape
  - b. Aug. 6, 1843, Lautto, Sweden
- c) Anna Brita Alexandersdotter Makikokko
  - b. Dec. 28, 1844, Ylimuonio, Muonionniska fs, Finland
- d) Karl Alexander Lantto
  - b. Aug. 7, 1846, Ylimuonio, Finland
- e) Aapo Abram Lantto
  - b. Nov. 15, 1848
- f) Mattia Isaak Lantto
  - b. Sept. 7, 1850, Ylimuonio, Finland
- g) Matilda Alexandersdotter Makikokko
  - b. June 3, 1853, Ylimuonio, Muonionniska, fs, Finland

8) Johan Matthias Lantto

- b. Feb. 28, 1841, Yliumuonio, Finland
- d. March 25, 1889, French Lake, MN
- m. Maria Lovisa Jerisjarvi
  - b. Nov. 17, 1838, Alamuonio, Muonionniska fs, Finland
  - d. April 28, 1928, Wright Co., MN

Children: (all born in Ylimuonio, Finland)
- a) Mary Emily Lantto
  - b. Jan. 27, 1866
- b) Maria Elmina Lantto
  - b. Jan. 27, 1866
- c) Johan (John) Alexander Lantto
  - b. Oct. 28, 1868
- d) Greta Matilda Lantto
  - b. Dec. 20, 1870
- e) Jacob Lantto

b. Oct. 14, 1872
f) Abraham Lantto
b. Dec. 1, 1874
g) Ida Sofia Lantto
b. Jan. 6, 1880

*Johan Matthias and Maria Lovisa Lantto came to USA in 1881.

9) Jacob Lantto

b. Oct. 14, 1872, Ylimuonio, Finland
d. June 15, 1946, French Lake, MN
m. Olga Mary Mattson
    b. July 21, 1883, Finland
    d. Nov. 4, 1918, Cokato, MN
Children from Olga Mary Mattson Lantto:
a) Lillian Mary Sofia Lantto Barberg
    b. Jan. 28, 1904, West Albion, MN
    d. July 3, 1981, Cokato, MN
    m. Wayne Barberg (1900-1968)
b) Alfred Jacob Lantto
    b. May 5, 1905, West Albion, MN
    d. Nov. 16, 1972, Belden, ND
    m. Ellen Lahtinen (1901-1994)
c) Ida Olive Lantto Schroeder
    b. June 22, 1906, West Albion, MN
    d. May 19, 1996, Detroit Lakes, MN
    m. Francis C. Schroeder (1906-1987)
d) Mark Lantto
    b. Aug. 11, 1908, French Lake, MN
    d. May 20, 1975, Minneapolis, MN
e) Mildred Evelyn Lantto Maki Walker
    b. Dec. 24, 1910, French Lake, MN
    d. Sept. 1989/1990

f) Ansel Francis Lantto
   b. May 29, 1911, French Lake, MN
   d. Oct. 18, 1955, Belden, ND
g) Anna Lantto
   b. 1912
   d. 1912, French Lake, MN
h) Reino Harold Lantto
   b. Jan. 21, 1914, French Lake, MN
   d. Jan. 18, 1990, Annandale, MN
   m. Elaine Mabel Tormanen
i) Erving Mathew Lantto
   b. Oct. 6, 1916, French Lake, MN
   d. Minneapolis, MN
   m. Josephine Zwyzacka
j) Beatrice Louise Lantto Lusti
   b. Jan/June 1, 1917, French Lake, MN
   d. 1990
   m. Vernon Lusti
      b. Jan. 23, 1916
k) Eddie Lantto
   b. Nov. 4, 1918
   d. Nov. 4, 1918, Cokato, MN
m. Anna Nikka Matsen
Anna Nikka Matsen's children prior to marrying Jacob Lantto:
      a) Edwin Matsen
      b) Viola Matsen
      c) Virgil Matsen
      d) Harold Matsen
Jacob and Anna Matsen Lantto's children:
   a) Rachel Lantto Walberg
      m. Lloyd Walberg
   b) Leo Lantto
      m. Leona

c) Calvin Lantto
   m. Betty Smith
d) Betty Lantto Lambert
   m. Clinton Lambert
e) Kenneth Lantto
   m. Barbara McChesney

Ida Lantto Schroeder's Father's (Jacob Lantto)
Maternal Genealogy
(Nine Generations)

1) Anund nn
    b. 1590
    d. unknown, in Finland
  m. unknown
Children:
Anund Anundsson

2) Anund Anundsson
    b. circa 1620, in Muonioiska, Muonio, Finland
    d. unknown
  m. Brita nn
        b. circa 1620
        d. unknown
Children:
Hans Anundsson Katkasuando (aka Anundinpoika)
        b. 1650

3) Hans Anundsson Katkasuando
    b. 1650 in Muonionniska, Finland
    d. unknown
  m. Anna nn
        b. circa 1648, in Finland or Sweden
        d. unknown
Children:
    a) Henrik Hansson Katkasuando (aka Hansinpoika)
          b. circa 1667 in Katkasuando, Muonio, Finland
          d. 1734 in Muonen Niska, Overtornio, Finland

m. Margret Ersdotter
Children:
  a) Mats Henrikson Katkasuando
       b. 1700
  b) Henrik Hindersson Katkasuando
       b. 1703
  c) Regina Henriksdotter Katkasuando
       b. 1708
b) Jons Hansson Katkasuando
     b. 1670

4) Jons Hansson Katkasuando
     b. 1670
     d. 1709
  m. Marit Katkasuando
  Children:
  a) Carin (Karin) (Catharina) Jonsdotter Katkasuando
       b. 1685, Muonio, Finland
  b) Johan Johansson Vountisjarvi (aka Jons Jonsson, or Juho Juhonpoikam)
       b. 1696, Muonionniska, Finland
  c) Anna Katkasuando
       b. unknown

5) Johan Johansson Vountisjarvi (aka Jons Jonsson, or Juho Juhonpoikam Johan Johansson Vountisjarvi)
     b. 1696, Muonionniska, Finland
     d. July 25, 1775, in Finland
  m. Margareta Nilsdotter Kunnari (Kunnare)
  Children:
  a) Marget Johansdotter Vountisjarvi
       b. March 23, 1747, Vountisjarvi, Enontekio fs, Finland
  b) Nils Johansson Nilmaa

b. Aug. 9, 1749, Vountisjarvi, Enontekio sk, Finland

c) Per Johansson Vountisjarvi

b. March 25, 1751, Suondavaara, Enontekio fs, Finland

d) Hindrick Johansson Vountisjarvi

b. May 29, 1753

e) Thomas Johansson Vountisjarvi

b. Jan. 20, 1757

f) Olof Jonsson Jerisjarvi

b. Nov. 12, 1759, Enontekio fs, Finland

g) Ella Johansdotter Vountisjarvi

b. Jan. 23, 1762

6) Olof Jonsson Jerisjarvi (aka Olof Jonsson Vountisjarvi)

b. Nov. 12, 1759, Vountisjarvi, Enontekio fs, Finland

d. Nov. 20, 1817 in Muonionniska, Finland

m. Eva Johansdotter Niva

b. unknown

Children:

a) Johan Olofsson Niemela

b. 1793 in Alamuonio, Muonioniska sk, Finland

b) Eva Olofsdotter Jerisjarvi

b. 1795 in Muonionniska fs, Finland

c) Olof Olofsson Jerisjarvi

b. 1796 in Muonionniska fs, Finland

d) Anna Greta Olofsdotter Jerisjarvi

b. 1797 in Alamuonio, Muonioniska fs, Finland

e) Abram Olofsson Jerisjarvi

b. Oct. 4, 1799 in Muonionniska fs, Finland

f) Isak Ollinpoika Jerisjarvi

b. July 7, 1802 in Alamuonio, Muonioniska sk, Finland

g) Gabriel Olofsson

b.   July 22, 1807
h) Joel Olofsson Kutuniva
  b.   Oct. 18, 1808 in Alamuonio, Muonioniska fs,
     Finland

7) Isak Ollinpoika Jerisjarvi

b.   July 7, 1802 in Alamuonio, Muonioniska sk, Finland
d.   March 2, 1892 in Alamuonio, Muonioniska sk, Finland
m. Ella Maria Juhontytar Olli
  b.   unknown
Children: (all born in Alamuonio, Muonioniska sk, Finland)
a) Anna Greta Jerisjarvi
  b.   April 11, 1831
b) Eva Stina Jerisjarvi
  b.   Oct. 1, 1833
c) Brita Kaisa Lisakintytar Jerisjarvi
  b.   Feb. 26, 1836
d) Maria Lovisa Jerisjarvi
  b.   Nov. 17, 1838
e) Magdalena Lisakintytar Jerisjarvi
  b.   Sept. 4, 1840
f) Juho Aapo Lisakinpoika Jerisjarvi
  b.   June 6, 1843
g) Sofia Henrika Jerisjarvi
  b.   Jan. 23, 1846
h) Isak Jerisjarvi
  b.   March 6, 1849
i) Joel Isaksson Ranta
  b.   June 30, 1851

8) Maria Lovisa Jerisjarvi

b. Nov. 17, 1838 in Alamuonio, Muonioniska sk, Finland

d. April 28, 1928 in French Lake, Wright Co., Minnesota

m. Johan Matthais Lantto and Jacob Keranen Jacobson

Children from Johan Matthias Lantto (all born in Ylimuonio, Finland)

a) Mary Emily Lantto

    b. Jan. 27, 1866

b) Maria Elmina Lantto

    b. Jan. 27, 1866

c) Johan (John) Alexander Lantto

    b. Oct. 28, 1868

d) Greta Matilda Lantto

    b. Dec. 20, 1870

e) Jacob Lantto

    b. Oct. 14, 1872

f) Abraham Lantto

    b. Dec. 1, 1874

g) Ida Sofia Lantto

    b. Jan. 6, 1880

9) Jacob Lantto

b. Oct. 14, 1872 in Ylimuonio, Finland

d. June 15, 1946, in French Lake, MN

m. Olga Mary Mattson

    b. July 21, 1883 in Finland

    d. Nov. 4, 1918, Cokato, MN

Children from Olga Mary Mattson:

a) Lillian Mary Sofia Lantto Barberg

    b. Jan. 28, 1904, West Albion, MN

    d. July 3, 1981, Cokato, MN

    m. Wayne Barberg (1900-1968)

b) Alfred Jacob Lantto
   - b. May 5, 1905, West Albion, MN
   - d. Nov. 16, 1972, Belden, ND
   - m. Ellen Lahtinen (1901-1994)
c) Ida Olive Lantto Schroeder
   - b. June 22, 1906, West Albion, MN
   - d. May 19, 1996, Detroit Lakes, MN
   - m. Francis C. Schroeder (1906-1987)
d) Mark Lantto
   - b. Aug. 11, 1908, French Lake, MN
   - d. May 20, 1975, Minneapolis, MN
e) Mildred Evelyn Lantto Maki Walker
   - b. Dec. 24, 1910, French Lake, MN
   - d. Sept. 1989/90
f) Ansel Francis Lantto
   - b. May 29, 1911, French Lake, MN
   - d. Oct. 18, 1955, Belden, ND (buried in French Lake)
g) Anna Lantto
   - b. 1912, French Lake, MN
   - d. 1912
h) Reino Harold Lantto
   - b. Jan. 21, 1914, French Lake, MN
   - d. Jan. 18, 1990, Annandale, MN
   - m. Elaine Mabel Tormanen
i) Erving Mathew Lantto
   - b. Oct. 6, 1916, French Lake, MN
   - d. Minneapolis, MN
   - m. Josephine Zwyzacka
j) Beatrice Louise Lantto Lusti
   - b. Jan/June 1, 1917, French Lake, MN
   - d. 1990
   - m. Vernon Lusti
       - b. Jan. 23, 1916

k) Eddie Lantto

      b. Nov. 4, 1918

      d. Nov. 4, 1918

m. Anna Nikka Matsen

Anna Nikka Matsen's children prior to marrying Jacob:

a) Edwin Matsen

b) Viola Matsen

c) Virgil Matsen

d) Harold Matsen

Jacob and Anna Matsen Lantto's children:

a) Rachel Lantto Walberg

    m. Lloyd Walberg

b) Leo Lantto

    m. Leona

c) Calvin Lantto

    m. Betty Smith

d) Betty Lantto

    m. Clinton Lambert

e) Kenneth Lantto

    m. Barbara McChesney

Olga Mary Mattson Lantto
Paternal Genealogy
(Three Generations)

1) Matti Mattson
>   b. (est) 1790-1850
>   d. unknown
> m. unknown
> Children:
>   Mat (Matti) Mattsson Mattson
>   b.   Feb. 8, 1855

2) Mat (Matti) Mattsson Mattson
>   b.   Feb. 8, 1855 in Finland
>   d.   July 18, 1914, Corrinna, Wright Co., MN
> m. Beatrice Sophia Backman Mattson
>   (Beatrice also married Joseph Davidson
>   b.   1849, Finland
>   d.   Dec. 7, 1938, Cokato, MN)
>   b.   April 1855, Finland
>   d.   Aug. 3, 1947 in Lynden, Stearns Co., MN
> Children:
>   a) Olga Mary Mattson
>   b.   July 21, 1883, Finland
>   d.   Nov. 4, 1918, Cokato, MN
>   b) John M. Matson
>   b. May 1887, Finland
>   c) Olive (Alley) S. Matson Miller
>   b.   Nov. 15, 1890, Calumet, MI
>   d.   Dec. 26, 1967, Hennepin Co., MN
>   m. Gustavus (Gus) Miller (1882-1969)

d) Francis (Frank) Matson
  b. May 1, 1894, Calumet, MI

3) Olga Mary Mattson Lantto

  b. July 21, 1883, Finland
  d. Nov. 4, 1918, Cokato, MN
m. Jacob F. Lantto
  b. Oct. 14, 1872, Ylimuonio, Finland
Children:

  a) Lillian Mary Sofia Lantto Barberg
    b. Jan. 28, 1904, West Albion, MN
    d. July 3, 1981, Cokato, MN
    m. Wayne Barberg (1900-1968)

  b) Alfred Jacob Lantto
    b. May 5, 1905, West Albion, MN
    d. Nov. 16, 1972, Belden, ND
    m. Ellen Lahtinen (1901-1994)

  c) Ida Olive Lantto Schroeder
    b. June 22, 1906, West Albion, MN
    d. May 19, 1996, Detroit Lakes, MN
    m. Francis Schroeder (1906-1987)

  d) Mark Lantto
    b. Aug. 11, 1908, French Lake, MN
    d. May 20, 1975, Minneapolis, MN

  e) Mildred Evelyn Lantto Maki Walker
    b. Dec. 24, 1910, French Lake, MN
    d. Sept. 1889/1990

  f) Ansel Francis Lantto
    b. May 29, 1911, French Lake, MN
    d. Oct. 18, 1955, Belden, ND

  g) Anna Lantto
    b. 1912
    d. 1912, French Lake, MN

h) Reino Harold Lantto
   - b. Jan. 21, 1914, French Lake, MN
   - d. Jan. 18, 1990, Annandale, MN
   - m. Elaine Mabel Tormanen
i) Erving Mathew Lantto
   - b. Oct. 6, 1916, French Lake, MN
   - d. Minneapolis, MN
   - m. Josephine Zwyzacka
j) Beatrice Louise Lantto Lusti
   - b. Jan/June 1917, French Lake, MN
   - d. 1990
   - m. Vernon Lusti
      - b. Jan. 23, 1916
k) Eddie Lantto
   - b. Nov. 4, 1918
   - d. Nov. 4, 1918, Cokato, MN

www.ingramcontent.com/pod-product-compliance
Lightning Source LLC
Chambersburg PA
CBHW071844090426
42811CB00035B/2322/J